OKLAHOMA

OKLAHOMA

HELLO
U.S.A.

by Rita C. LaDoux

Lerner Publications Company

You'll find this picture of an Indian blanket flower at the beginning of each chapter in this book. Oklahoma's state wildflower, Indian blanket blooms in June and July and is found throughout the state. The flower is usually red with yellow tips. Indian blanket is a symbol of Oklahoma's scenic beauty and Indian heritage.

Cover (left): Cache Creek in the Wichita Mountains. Cover (right): Sculpture of a bull's head at the entrance to the Oklahoma National Stockyards in Oklahoma City. Pages 2–3: Oil well. Page 3: Oklahoma City.

This book is available in two editions:
Library binding by Lerner Publications Company, a division of Lerner Publishing Group
Soft cover by First Avenue Editions, an imprint of Lerner Publishing Group
241 First Avenue North
Minneapolis, MN 55401 U.S.A.

Website address: www.lernerbooks.com

Library of Congress Cataloging-in-Publication Data

LaDoux, Rita, 1951–
    Oklahoma / by Rita C. LaDoux (Rev. and expanded 2nd ed.)
        p.   cm. — (Hello U.S.A.)
    Summary: An introduction to the land, history, people, economy, and
        environment of Oklahoma.
    Includes bibliographical references and index.
    ISBN: 0–8225–4098–3 (lib. bdg. : alk paper)
    ISBN: 0–8225–0791–9 (pbk. : alk paper)
    1. Oklahoma—Juvenile literature. [1. Oklahoma.] I. Title. II. Series.
    F694.3.L34 2003
    976.6—dc21   2002005526

Manufactured in the United States of America
1 2 3 4 5 6 – JR – 08 07 06 05 04 03

CONTENTS

This unusual rock formation in the Oklahoma Panhandle is often called the Wedding Party.

THE LAND

Plains and Plateau

The state of Oklahoma takes its name from two Choctaw Indian words, *okla* (people) and *homma* (red). Oklahoma lies in the south central United States. Four states—Texas, New Mexico, Colorado, and Kansas—surround the Oklahoma Panhandle, a long, narrow strip of land that extends west from northwestern Oklahoma. Texas (to the south) and Kansas (to the north) continue all the way to Oklahoma's eastern border. There, Oklahoma meets Missouri and Arkansas.

Oklahoma has many different landforms. But the state can be divided into five geographic regions. They are the Ozark Plateau, the Arkansas Valley, the Ouachita Mountains, the Red River Region, and the Western Plains.

Northeastern Oklahoma has rushing rivers and gently flowing streams.

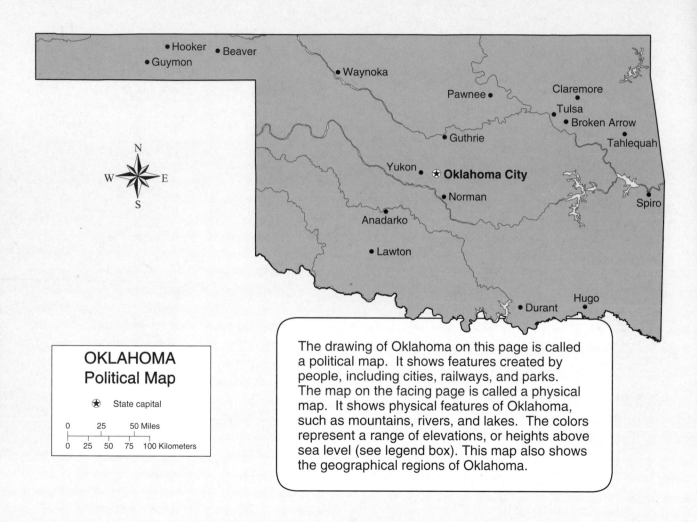

OKLAHOMA
Political Map

⊛ State capital

0   25   50 Miles

0 25 50 75 100 Kilometers

The drawing of Oklahoma on this page is called a political map. It shows features created by people, including cities, railways, and parks. The map on the facing page is called a physical map. It shows physical features of Oklahoma, such as mountains, rivers, and lakes. The colors represent a range of elevations, or heights above sea level (see legend box). This map also shows the geographical regions of Oklahoma.

Map labels:
• Hooker
• Beaver
• Guymon
• Waynoka
Pawnee •
Claremore
• Tulsa
• Broken Arrow
Tahlequah
• Guthrie
Yukon • ⊛ Oklahoma City
• Norman
Spiro
• Anadarko
• Lawton
Hugo
• Durant

N W E S

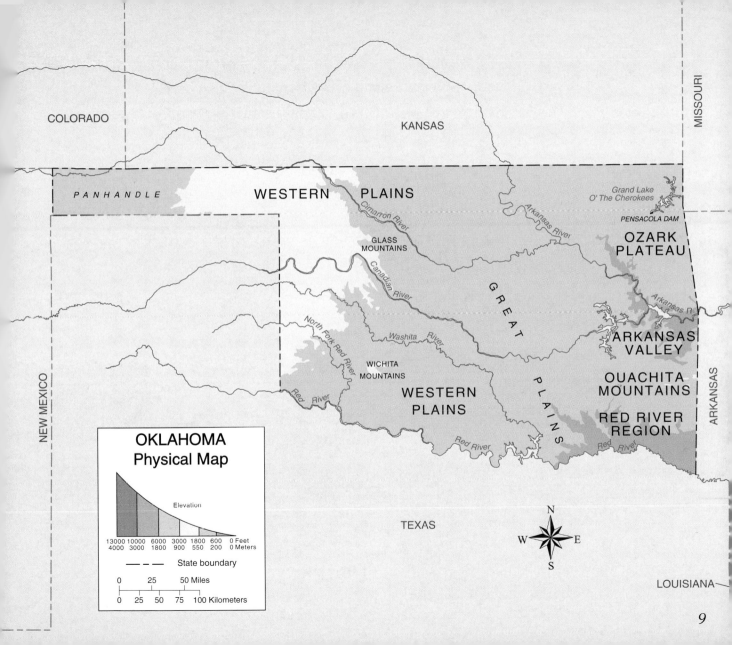

COLORADO

KANSAS

MISSOURI

PANHANDLE

WESTERN PLAINS

Cimarron River

Grand Lake
O' The Cherokees

PENSACOLA DAM

OZARK
PLATEAU

GLASS
MOUNTAINS

Arkansas River

Canadian River

G R E A T

Arkansas R.

NEW MEXICO

North Fork Red River

Washita River

WICHITA
MOUNTAINS

Arkansas R.

ARKANSAS
VALLEY

P L A I N S

OUACHITA
MOUNTAINS

ARKANSAS

Red River

WESTERN
PLAINS

RED RIVER
REGION

Red River

Red River

OKLAHOMA
Physical Map

Elevation

| 13000 | 10000 | 6000 | 3000 | 1800 | 600 | 0 Feet |
| 4000 | 3000 | 1800 | 900 | 550 | 200 | 0 Meters |

– – – State boundary

0   25   50 Miles

0   25   50   75   100 Kilometers

TEXAS

N
W   E
S

LOUISIANA

9

The hills of the Ozark Plateau roll into northeastern Oklahoma from Missouri and Arkansas. Millions of years ago, underground pressures pushed this region above the land around it, creating a high **plateau.** Rushing rivers have cut deep valleys into the plateau.

The Arkansas Valley, a region covered by grassy plains and forested hills, is south and west of the Ozark Plateau. The Arkansas River runs southeast through the valley toward Arkansas.

South of the Arkansas Valley lie the Ouachita Mountains, the most rugged region in the state. Spring-fed rivers carve through the region's low valleys, and forests blanket the mountains' high ridges.

The Red River winds slowly through the Red River Region. At one time, the river regularly flooded the surrounding plains after heavy rains. Although floods still occur, dams keep the river

The Ouachita Mountains are located in southeastern Oklahoma.

Rugged hills spring up on Oklahoma's Western Plains *(left)*. The hills are called the Glass Mountains because they're covered with shiny layers of the mineral gypsum. Wide, grassy prairies cover parts of the Western Plains *(below)*.

from overflowing as often as it used to. Peanuts and cotton are raised in the Red River Region.

The Western Plains stretch across the western two-thirds of Oklahoma, from the Red River Region to the end of the Panhandle. Mountains jut up from the southern part of the Western Plains, but low hills blanket most of the region. In the Panhandle, **mesas** (flat-topped hills) dot broad **prairies,** or grasslands. The Panhandle is also part of the Great Plains, a huge region that extends from Texas to Canada.

The Wichita Mountains rise in southwestern Oklahoma.

Two large rivers, the Red and the Arkansas, flow through Oklahoma. The Red River forms Oklahoma's southern border with Texas. Rivers in southern Oklahoma, including the Washita and the North Fork, pour into the Red River. The Canadian, Cimarron, and several other rivers feed the Arkansas River, which runs through northeastern Oklahoma.

The state has some natural lakes, but people created its largest lakes when they built dams to block the flow of rivers. The water released through some of these dams spins engines that create **hydroelectric power.** This power fuels lights and machines in homes and businesses.

Swimmers frolic under Turner Falls, a waterfall in the Western Plains.

In the skies over Oklahoma, cold air flowing south from Canada runs into warm, moist air flowing north from the Gulf of Mexico. This makes Oklahoma's weather very quick to change. Strong winds often blow across the state, and violent tornadoes sometimes twist through the area in the spring and summer.

A tornado roars through the Oklahoma prairie.

Snow blankets a park in Oklahoma City.

Temperatures and rainfall can change a lot from day to day, but most of Oklahoma is usually warm and dry. Summer temperatures average 82° F, but they sometimes climb as high as 120° F. Winter temperatures generally stay above freezing. The Panhandle gets only about 15 inches of rain and snow each year, but the muggy Red River Region can get more than 50 inches a year.

Oklahomans looking for wildlife might spot an armadillo *(right)* or a prairie dog *(below)*.

Short prairie grasses grow throughout the dry western half of Oklahoma. This was once grazing land for huge herds of buffalo, and it is still home to smaller animals—coyotes, armadillos, rabbits, and prairie dogs.

Tall prairie grasses once waved over the plains of eastern Oklahoma. Much of this land has been planted with crops. In the eastern hills, pine, pecan, walnut, sweet gum, and oak trees grow. These forests provide homes and food for deer, opossums, raccoon, mink, squirrels, and foxes.

THE HISTORY

Natives and Newcomers

he earliest people in what became Oklahoma came to the area more than 10,000 years ago. These Native Americans, or Indians, lived on the plains and hunted buffalo and mastodons—huge animals that looked like hairy elephants.

By A.D. 600, another group of Indians had moved into the region. These Indians are called mound builders because they built large earthen mounds, or hills. The Indians buried their dead in some of these mounds and worshiped the sun and the four seasons on top of other mounds.

To get close to a buffalo herd, Plains Indians in Oklahoma sometimes disguised themselves in wolf skins.

The mound builders lived in a town near what later became Spiro, Oklahoma. Some of their burial and temple mounds still stand.

The mound builders planted fields of corn, squash, and tobacco in the fertile Arkansas Valley. No one knows what happened to these people. Dry weather in the 1300s may have caused their crops to fail. If so, they probably starved to death or moved away in search of food.

Europeans knew little about the land where the mound builders once lived. Some believed Indians lived in cities of gold. In 1541 Spanish explorer Francisco Vásquez de Coronado searched North America for these golden cities. Instead of gold, Coronado found groups of Indians who lived in small villages, hunted buffalo, and grew corn.

When Francisco Vásquez de Coronado arrived in the Oklahoma area, he met groups of Wichita Indians. The Indians lived in grass houses like this one, which was built in the 1800s.

Plains Indians used buffalo in many ways. They carved buffalo bones into tools, made clothes and tepees out of the skins, and cooked the meat over fires fueled by dried buffalo dung.

Coronado discovered no riches for himself in North America, but he and other explorers left a treasure for the Indians—horses. With horses, Indians could leave their fields to ride after the millions of buffalo on the Great Plains.

Soon the Cheyenne, Comanche, Kiowa, Osage, Pawnee, Wichita, and other Indian tribes were hunting buffalo in the Oklahoma area. These groups spoke many different languages and had different customs, but all of them hunted buffalo and lived on the Great Plains. They became known as the Plains Indians.

The Plains Indians did not know it, but in 1682 France claimed their hunting grounds. France made them part of Louisiana, a vast piece of land in North America. In 1803 France sold Louisiana to the United States in a deal called the Louisiana Purchase.

At the same time, many Europeans were sailing to the United States. As the country grew more crowded, its citizens wanted more land. Some wanted land in the southeastern United States that belonged to five different Indian groups—the Choctaw, Chickasaw, Cherokee, Creek, and Seminole.

To make more room for the new settlers, the U.S. government pushed these Indians west. In the 1830s, the five groups were forced to move to a part of Louisiana called the Indian Territory. This territory covered parts of what became Oklahoma, Kansas, and Nebraska.

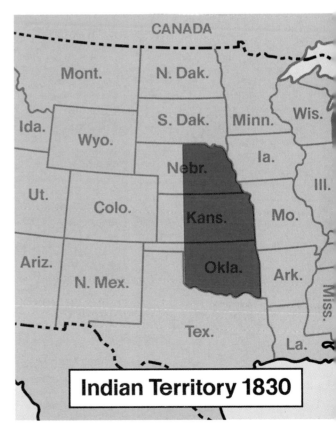

Indian Territory 1830

The Trail of Tears

The trip from the southeastern United States to Oklahoma was long and hard for the Choctaw, Chickasaw, Cherokee, Creek, and Seminole Indians. Some groups of Indians were taken west to Oklahoma in old, unsafe steamboats or wagons. Other groups were forced to walk thousands of miles to their new homes. The Indians were often moved in the winter, but they were not given shoes, warm clothing, or enough food. Many people suffered from frostbite. Others starved, froze, or died of disease. So many Indians died during the Cherokee removal of 1838 *(depicted above)* that the journey became known as the Trail of Tears.

The Choctaw, Chickasaw, Cherokee, Creek, and Seminole Indians did not live like the Plains Indians. For example, the five groups built many of their buildings, such as the Choctaw council house *(left)*, in the style of the buildings of European settlers.

The land that became Oklahoma was divided among the five groups. Each governed its own nation and made its own laws. The Indians built towns and farms and opened schools.

Just as they had in their former homes, some Indians built **plantations** (large farms) and used black slaves to work in the fields. The use of slaves throughout the southern United States was causing many arguments. Northern lawmakers wanted to outlaw slavery. But southerners wanted slaves to work on their plantations. These differences led to the Civil War, or the war between the North and the South, which broke out in 1861.

Since Indians were often not allowed to leave their reservations to hunt, many groups depended on the U.S. government for food. These Cheyenne Indians wait for their flour, sugar, and meat.

In 1865 the North won the Civil War. The Union (North) punished everyone in the Indian Territory whether they had fought for the South or not. The territory was reduced to the area that later became Oklahoma. The government squeezed the five groups into the eastern half of this territory. Then the government moved some of the Plains Indians, as well as tribes from all over the country, to **reservations** (land reserved for Indians) in the western part of the Indian Territory.

As more tribes moved into the Indian Territory, so did white people. Between 1866 and 1885, cowboys drove more than 6 million longhorn cattle from Texas across Oklahoma.

Next came the railroads. In the 1870s, workers laid track across Oklahoma for the Missouri-Kansas-Texas Railroad. Shopkeepers set up stores along the tracks, and towns grew up around the stores.

With the cowboys, railroads, and towns came the end of the Indians' way of life. Many cowboys drove cattle across Indian land without asking permission. Cattlemen rented vast pieces of land from the Indians for some of Oklahoma's first cattle ranches.

Cowboys drove their cattle across Oklahoma. They took the animals to Kansas, where the animals were shipped to markets in the east.

Buffalo destroyed train tracks and slowed trains. Railroad builders sent hunters out to shoot the animals.

White hunters also destroyed one of the Indians' sources of food by shooting huge numbers of buffalo. Hunters skinned the animals and left their bodies to rot on the Great Plains. By 1885 millions of buffalo had been killed, and only a small number were left.

Another threat to the Indians came from the east. By the 1880s, settlers had spread throughout much of the United States. Most farmland across the country had been claimed. People thought the Indian Territory was the last place left to get their own land. Settlers called Boomers hurried to the territory, hoping to "boom" onto Indian land.

The U.S. Army forced the Boomers to leave the territory, which still belonged to Indian tribes. But Boomer leaders convinced the government to buy a small piece of land, called the Unassigned Lands, from the Indians. Settlers would be allowed to move onto this land on April 22, 1889.

In 1889 some settlers snuck onto the Indian Territory and illegally claimed the best land before it was opened for settlement. They were called Sooners, because they arrived too soon. Here, soldiers force some Sooners to leave the territory.

At noon on April 22, 1889, the Land Run began. More than 50,000 settlers raced in wagons, on horses, or on foot to claim plots of land. By the end of the day, the cities of Guthrie and Oklahoma City had sprung up and grown to more than 8,000 people each.

Black families were among the settlers who claimed land in the Land Run.

Settlers race to claim land in the town of Guthrie *(left)*. New buildings sprang up on Guthrie's main street *(below)* immediately after the Land Run.

These maps show how the Indian Territory dwindled from 1870 to 1890.

So many settlers moved to the Indian Territory in 1889 that the U.S. government divided it in half. The eastern half was still the Indian Territory, owned by Indian tribes. The western half, including the Unassigned Lands, became the Oklahoma Territory.

The Oklahoma Territory's new settlers soon wanted more of the Indians' land. The government took each tribe's land and divided it into separate plots, called allotments. Each tribe member got a small plot. But the government made more plots than there were tribe members. Then the government bought the leftover land and gave it to new settlers who poured into the Oklahoma Territory.

Not all of the newcomers wanted farmland. Some of them wanted to mine the oil that had been discovered beneath Oklahoma's soil. Oil was needed to fuel homes and factories. Mining grew, along with ranching and farming, as railroads carried Oklahoma's products to markets on the country's East Coast. Railroads also brought more **immigrants** (newcomers) to the territory from the eastern United States and from Europe.

As the Oklahoma Territory's population of new settlers grew, many people wanted the region to become a state. People living in the Indian Territory wanted their territory to be a separate state called Sequoyah. But the U.S. government decided to admit both territories as one state. On November 16, 1907, the two territories became Oklahoma, the 46th state. In this new state, fewer than one out of every five people was an American Indian.

Large amounts of oil lay underground in Oklahoma in the early 1900s. Some wells gushed for days before workers could stop them.

The Osage Indians became rich after oil was discovered on their land. In fact, some became millionaires during the oil boom of the 1920s.

Settlers kept coming to Oklahoma. Many of them hoped to strike it rich in the oil business. During the early 1920s, more oil was pumped in Oklahoma than any other state. Workers drilled thousands of wells. Many of the wells spewed so much oil, known as "black gold," that their owners made a fortune.

The Tulsa Race Riot

In 1921 a riot broke out in Tulsa after a group of whites threatened to kill a black man. The black man had been accused of attacking a white girl. Some African Americans gathered to protect him, and violence erupted. White rioters destroyed more than $1 million worth of buildings in the black community. At least 80 people—probably many more—were killed. Black Tulsans rebuilt most of their homes and businesses within a year.

In the 1930s, the Great Depression hit the United States, leaving many people out of jobs and short of money. Oil and beef prices dropped. Many businesses closed. Farmers had to sell their crops for very low prices.

By 1933 there were few crops left to sell. A severe **drought,** or dry spell, hit the Great Plains, drying

A farmer and his children seek shelter from the dust storm that is burying their shack. The severe drought of the 1930s brought hard times for many Oklahomans.

A dust cloud billows over the streets of Hooker, Oklahoma, in the 1930s.

the land and killing thousands of acres of crops. Farmers had cleared their fields of trees and plowed up prairie sod, leaving no roots to hold the state's soil in place. Oklahoma's strong winds whipped the dry, dusty soil into people's homes, food, and water. Clouds of dust five miles high blocked out the sun. Part of Oklahoma became known as the Dust Bowl.

Thousands of Oklahomans left their dried-up farms and headed to California, where they hoped to find jobs. When the drought finally ended in 1939, Oklahoma's farms were in bad shape. But people had started planting trees to block the wind, and farmers began growing crops with roots strong enough to hold down the soil.

By 1941 many farms had recovered. That same year, the United States entered World War II (1939–1945). The military needed wheat, beef, and oil. Farmers, ranchers, and oil drillers had plenty of work. Oklahomans built airfields and military bases in their state, where the flat land was ideal for training pilots and soldiers.

During World War II, many Oklahomans moved to cities, where people took jobs in factories to make supplies for the war. By the war's end in 1945, more people lived in cities than on farms. The state's larger cities, such as Oklahoma City and Tulsa, had grown up near oil and natural gas fields. Many businesses across the country needed these fuels to run machinery. As other states bought more oil and gas from Oklahoma, the state thrived.

After World War II, Oklahomans wanted to earn a living not only from oil and farm products. They built factories for goods such as plastics, electronics, and space equipment.

Oklahomans also worked on building dams on the state's rivers. The dams prevent floods and provide

hydroelectric power for the state. In 1970 the McClellan-Kerr Arkansas River Navigation System was completed. The project made the Arkansas River deeper and wider. Dams and locks were built on the river so that ships can travel all the way from the Gulf of Mexico to Oklahoma.

During the 1970s, Oklahoma's Native Americans won more power to govern their tribes. Indian groups also worked to regain some of their native land.

High demand for Oklahoma's oil made the state's economy boom during the late 1970s. But during the 1980s, oil prices fell. Prices of farm products also went down. Many Oklahomans lost their jobs. The state looked again to develop industries other than oil and farming—computer manufacturing, food distribution, and equipment rental.

After World War II, refineries were built in Oklahoma. Refineries clean oil before it is sent to factories.

The Alfred E. Murrah Federal Building in Oklahoma City was devastated by the April 1995 bombing.

On April 19, 1995, a bomb set off by terrorists blew up the Alfred E. Murrah Federal Building in Oklahoma City. One hundred sixty-eight people died and 500 more were injured. Two Americans, Timothy McVeigh and Terry Nichols, were convicted of the crime. McVeigh was executed in 2001.

Oklahomans were shocked by the tragedy, but they banded together to recover. To remember the victims of the blast, they created a memorial on the site of the federal building. The Oklahoma City National Memorial opened in 2001. Oklahomans hope the memorial will offer comfort to those who lost friends and family in the bombing and teach visitors about the terrible impact of violence.

PEOPLE & ECONOMY

Western Spirit

ore American Indians live in Oklahoma than in almost any other state. Members of more than 39 Indian nations make up about 8 percent of the state's population, or about 273,000 people. Many Indians live in cities and towns. Others live on reservations.

A Creek man dressed in traditional clothing is ready for a powwow.

Children dance at the Czech Festival in Yukon, Oklahoma.

About 76 percent of all Oklahomans have European ancestors. Nearly 8 percent of Oklahomans are African American. About 5 percent are Latino, and 1 percent are Asian American.

Most of Oklahoma's 3.5 million people live in **urban** areas (cities) in the eastern part of the state. Oklahoma's two largest cities are Tulsa, a center for the production of oil and airplanes, and Oklahoma City, the state capital. Norman, Lawton, and Broken Arrow are the next largest cities.

Compared to some other states, Oklahoma doesn't have many big urban areas, and much of the state is still **rural** (countryside). In the Panhandle, miles of prairie separate farms and towns.

About 393,000 Oklahomans live in Tulsa.

Indian culture is important to many Oklahomans. At Tsa-La-Gi Ancient Village near Tahlequah, Cherokee Indians demonstrate how their people built villages and farmed before Europeans came to North America. At Anadarko, the Southern Plains Indian Museum displays arts and crafts of the Plains Indians. Dancers and drummers gather in Anadarko each August for the American Indian Exposition, one of the largest powwows in the United States.

At Tsa-La-Gi, Cherokee Indians make tools the way their ancestors did. They carve spears from stone and wood.

A statue in Oklahoma City honors Buffalo Bill Cody.

At the Gilcrease Museum in Tulsa and at the National Cowboy and Western Heritage Museum in Oklahoma City, visitors can view both Western and Indian art. History buffs can tour the town of Guthrie, which looks much like it did when Oklahoma was a new state. And at a museum in Claremore, comedian Will Rogers is remembered for his funny sayings and writings.

Oklahoma sports fans have plenty of games to choose from. Professional teams in the state include the Tulsa Oilers and Oklahoma City Blazers, hockey teams that play with the Central Hockey League. For many football fans, the game between Oklahoma State University and the University of Oklahoma is the sports highlight of the year.

Horses are popular in Oklahoma—whether for a relaxing ride *(above)* or a rough one. This rider *(right)* clings to his horse at a rodeo in Guymon.

The state is known for horses—rodeo horses, show horses, and racehorses. Professional riders rope cattle and ride broncos at rodeos all over Oklahoma. Horses race at Remington Park in Oklahoma City and parade at the World Championship Quarter Horse Show.

Oklahomans enjoy swimming, waterskiing, fishing, and boating on the state's many lakes. Deer, ducks, and wild turkeys attract hunters each fall. Dune-buggy drivers race at Little Sahara State Park. And hikers and campers explore hills and caves in the state's parks and forests.

There's lots to do in Oklahoma. People can go fishing *(above)* or zooming over sand dunes *(left)*.

Some Oklahomans take to the sky for their recreation. The state has hot-air ballooning clubs and hosts several balloon festivals each year.

Soldiers fire a practice round at Fort Sill.

Just as Oklahomans enjoy many different kinds of recreation, they also work at many different jobs. The largest number of Oklahoma's workers— 60 percent—have service jobs, or jobs helping other people or businesses. Bankers, salespeople, and doctors perform service jobs.

Oklahomans who work at military bases, such as Fort Sill and Tinker Air Force Base, have government jobs. Teachers in public schools and park rangers also work for the government.

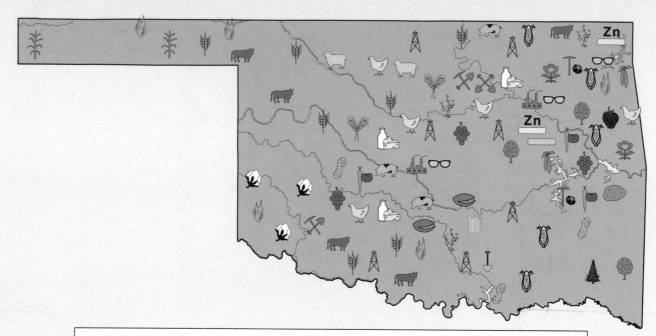

OKLAHOMA
Economic Map

The symbols on this map show where different economic activities take place in Oklahoma. The legend below explains what each symbol stands for.

Barley	Corn	Grapes	Natural gas	Pecans	Soybeans
Beef cattle	Cotton	Hay	Nursery products	Potatoes	Stone
Berries	Dairy products	Hogs	Oats	Poultry	Tourism
Clay	Forest products	Lead	Oil	Sand and gravel	Vegetables
Coal	Fruit	Manufacturing	Peanuts	Sheep	Wheat
				Sorghum	Zn Zinc

After services, manufacturing earns most of the state's money. Mechanics build the machinery used to pump and refine (separate and clean) oil and natural gas. Other workers refine the oil and gas. At some factories, Oklahomans use refined oil to make tires and plastic products. Still other Oklahomans build engines and airplanes at plants in Tulsa.

Three percent of the state's workers are employed in mining, which earns 6 percent of the state's money. Oklahomans pump oil and gas from the state's 84,000 oil wells and 32,000 natural gas wells. Workers then pipe the oil and gas to other states, where the fuels supply energy for cars, homes, and factories. Oklahoma's miners also dig for coal and gypsum, a whitish mineral used in plaster and candy.

At a plant in Tulsa, workers finish an airplane wing.

The state's ranchers graze their cattle on Oklahoma's grasslands and then fatten the cows in feedlots before selling them to meatpacking plants.

Oklahoma's wide prairie is cattle-grazing country.

Wheat, the state's largest crop, grows on the northern and southwestern plains. Oklahoma farmers also raise hogs, chickens, cotton, peanuts, soybeans, pecans, and watermelons. Six percent of the state's workers farm and ranch.

Although Oklahoma has many industries, the oil and gas industry affects more Oklahomans than most others. When fuel prices are low, many workers lose their jobs and have little money to spend. But when oil and gas sell for high prices, more jobs open in the oil industry. People in this field earn high wages. When these workers have more money to spend, many Oklahomans—from salespeople to doctors—benefit.

THE ENVIRONMENT

Saving Fossil Fuels

In ancient times, seas and swamps covered much of Oklahoma. As the tiny plants and animals that lived in these areas died, they sank to the bottom and were slowly covered by rocks and soil. Over millions of years, the pressure of these layers of earth turned the dead plants and animals into natural resources called **fossil fuels.**

The passing centuries have left three kinds of fossil fuels in Oklahoma—oil, natural gas, and coal. Oklahomans mine and sell these fuels. People in Oklahoma and other states also use these energy sources to power their cars and heat their homes. Fossil fuels employ thousands of Oklahoma's workers and bring billions of dollars into the state. But Oklahoma's fossil fuels are limited.

Pumps pull oil from wells in Oklahoma.

Some natural resources can be renewed, or replaced. To make sure future generations don't run out of wood, for example, people can plant trees. But fossil fuels cannot be renewed. Once the fuels have been mined, they cannot be replaced. Over the last 100 years, miners have dug up much of what took millions of years to create.

A miner adjusts valves on a natural gas well.

Most of Oklahoma's fossil fuels have been found on the plains of central Oklahoma. Geologists continue to look for oil and gas there.

To find more fossil fuels in Oklahoma, **geologists**, or people who study the earth, inspect the state's land surface and underground rock for the familiar signs of oil, gas, or coal. The geologists then try to predict where more deposits of fuels will be found.

Miners sometimes inject steam into a well to loosen up the remaining oil.

Scientists have also developed ways to get more oil out of mines that were thought to be empty. For example, some miners shoot water or steam deep into these wells. The steam thins the oil and flushes it out of cracks in the well. Miners can also remove oil from shale, a type of rock that gives off oil when it is heated.

People in Tulsa bring their used car oil and antifreeze to a recycling drive.

To avoid using up Oklahoma's fossil fuels, many Oklahomans are trying to use less fuel rather than finding more deposits of fuel. Carpooling and driving cars that use less gas are two ways to save fuel. Oklahomans can save some of the energy needed to run air conditioners and furnaces by keeping their homes warmer in the summer and cooler in the winter.

Recycling also saves fossil fuels. Some people help collect and recycle plastic containers such as milk jugs, which are made from oil. Car oil can be cleaned and reused.

Oklahomans want to use their natural resources wisely. Conserving, or using less, and recycling will make the state's fossil fuels last longer. But Oklahomans are also concerned about making a living. As people use less fuel to conserve for the future, Oklahomans might have to find new sources of money. By working together, miners and conservers may also be able to save both jobs and fossil fuels for future Oklahomans.

Oklahomans want to reserve some of their state's resources for recreation. The enormous Black Mesa juts into the westernmost edge of the Oklahoma Panhandle. The area is protected as part of Black Mesa State Park.

ALL ABOUT OKLAHOMA

Fun Facts

Oklahoma's nickname is the Sooner State. It came from people who tried to claim land sooner than they were allowed during the Land Run of 1889. Those settlers were known as Sooners.

Two elephants ran away from a circus near Hugo, Oklahoma, in 1975. The elephants were able to hide in the area's thick woods for two weeks before they were found.

Oklahoma is a leading peanut-growing state—only a few other states produce more. A concrete peanut, claimed to be the world's largest peanut by the town of Durant, honors some of the state's peanut farmers.

The Dual Parking Meter Company set up the country's first parking meters in Oklahoma City on July 16, 1935. The charge for parking was a nickel.

Oklahoma is the only state in which wells have been set up to pump oil from the grounds of the state capitol.

In June the residents of Okmulgee, Oklahoma, welcome visitors to their annual Pecan Festival. The city holds world records for the largest pecan pie, pecan cookie, pecan brownie, and the world's biggest ice cream and cookie party.

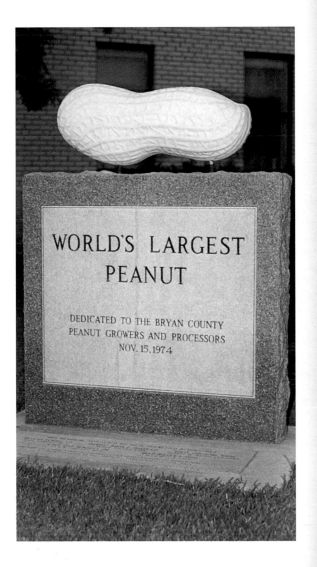

WORLD'S LARGEST PEANUT

DEDICATED TO THE BRYAN COUNTY
PEANUT GROWERS AND PROCESSORS
NOV. 15, 1974

STATE SONG

Oklahoma's state song is a famous one. It's the title song from the 1943 musical *Oklahoma!*, and it's great fun to sing.

OKLAHOMA!

Words and music by Richard Rodgers and Oscar Hammerstein

To hear "Oklahoma!" you can visit this website:
<http://www.otrd.state.ok.us/StudentGuide/emblems.html>

AN OKLAHOMA RECIPE

Oklahoma has an official state meal. It consists of fried okra, squash, cornbread, barbecue pork, biscuits, sausage and gravy, grits, corn, strawberries, chicken-fried steak, pecan pie, and black-eyed peas. Here's a basic recipe for an important part of the state meal.

CORNBREAD

1 cup buttermilk
1 cup stone-ground cornmeal
1 teaspoon salt

½ teaspoon baking soda
1 egg
1 tablespoon shortening

1. Ask an adult to preheat oven to 450° F.
2. Melt the shortening in 9-inch round iron skillet in the heating oven.
3. Stir cornmeal, salt, and baking soda together. Add egg and buttermilk. Mix well.
4. Ask an adult to remove skillet from the oven. Pour batter into skillet, stirring melted shortening into batter.
5. Bake for 30 to 40 minutes.
6. Ask an adult to remove pan from oven when top of cornbread is brown. Turn out onto a serving plate. Cut into wedges and serve immediately with butter.

HISTORICAL TIMELINE

8,000 B.C. Early Indians hunt mastodons in what later became Oklahoma.

A.D. 600 Mound builders settle near what later became Spiro.

1541 Francisco Vásquez de Coronado searches for golden cities.

1803 In a deal called the Louisiana Purchase, the United States buys from France the land that includes what later became Oklahoma.

1838 Cherokee Indians walk to Oklahoma in what became known as the Trail of Tears.

1861–1865 The Civil War takes place.

1866 Cowboys begin driving cattle across Oklahoma.

1870 Construction on the Missouri-Kansas-Texas Railroad begins in Oklahoma.

1889 The first Land Run begins.

1907 Oklahoma becomes the 46th state.

1921 A race riot erupts in Tulsa.

1929 The Great Depression begins.

1930s Dust storms and severe drought strike Oklahoma and the Great Plains.

1941 The United States enters World War II (1939–1945). Oklahomans provide food and supplies for the war effort, and soldiers train in the state.

1970 The McClellan-Kerr Arkansas River Navigation System is completed, boosting trade in Oklahoma.

1975 The Indian Self-Determination and Education Assistance Act gives tribal governments more power.

1995 The Alfred E. Murrah Federal Building in Oklahoma City is bombed, killing 168 people and injuring hundreds more.

1999 On May 3, tornadoes tear through central Oklahoma, killing 49 people and causing billions of dollars in damage.

2001 The Oklahoma City National Memorial opens in honor of the victims of the 1995 terrorist attack.

OUTSTANDING OKLAHOMANS

Cattle Annie (left) and Little Breeches

Louis W. Ballard (born 1931) is a composer who uses Native American themes in his music. He has written ballets and many pieces of music for orchestras. Ballard, a Quapaw-Cherokee Indian, was born on a reservation in Miami, Oklahoma.

Garth Brooks (born 1962) is a country musician. With albums like *Ropin' the Wind* and *No Fences*, Brooks helped make country music more popular. Born in Tulsa, Brooks is known for songs like "Friends in Low Places" and other hits.

The Bill Doolin Gang was famous in the 1890s for its many successful bank and train robberies. The gang's members included the young outlaws Cattle Annie and Little Breeches. One of the gang's favorite hideouts was in Ingalls, Oklahoma.

Angie Debo (1890–1988), a writer and historian, came to Oklahoma Territory in a covered wagon in 1899. She became an expert on Oklahoma history and wrote several books, including *Oklahoma: Foot-Loose and Fancy-Free.*

Ralph Waldo Ellison

Ralph Waldo Ellison (1914–1994) grew up in Oklahoma City. A teacher and writer, he was best known for his novel *Invisible Man,* which won the National Book Award in 1953.

Woody Guthrie (1912–1967) was a singer and composer born in Okemah, Oklahoma. Guthrie wrote more than 1,000 children's songs and folk songs, including "This Land Is Your Land."

Woody Guthrie

LaDonna Harris (born 1931) is the founder and president of Americans for Indian Opportunity, an organization that works to make tribal governments stronger. Harris, who is part Comanche, is from Lawton, Oklahoma.

Paul Harvey (born 1918), from Tulsa, Oklahoma, is a broadcast journalist for ABC News. His daily radio programs, "News and Comment" and "The Rest of the Story" are heard all over the country. Harvey also writes a newspaper column for the *Los Angeles Times*.

Ron Howard

Ron Howard (born 1954) is an actor and director from Duncan, Oklahoma. As a young actor, he starred in the popular television sitcoms *The Andy Griffith Show* (1960–1968) and *Happy Days* (1974–1984). Behind the camera, Howard has directed many movies, including, *Apollo 13* and *A Beautiful Mind*.

Jeane Jordan Kirkpatrick

Jeane Jordan Kirkpatrick (born 1926), from Duncan, Oklahoma, was the first woman to serve as the U.S. ambassador to the United Nations. Kirkpatrick teaches political science and has written several books about national and international politics.

Wilma Mankiller

Wilma Mankiller (born 1945) was the principal chief of the Cherokee Nation, the second largest tribe in the United States, from 1985 to 1995. She is the first woman to hold that office. Born in Stilwell, Oklahoma, Mankiller inherited her last name from a warrior ancestor.

Mickey Mantle (1931–1995) hit 536 home runs during his baseball career with the New York Yankees. Born in Spavinaw, Oklahoma, Mantle was named Most Valuable Player in the American League three times and was elected to the Baseball Hall of Fame in 1974.

Mickey Mantle

Reba McEntire (born 1955) is a popular country music singer. She has had many number-one hits and has starred in several movies. The daughter of a professional rodeo rider, McEntire was born in Chockie, Oklahoma.

N. Scott Momaday

N. Scott Momaday (born 1934) is a writer and teacher from Lawton, Oklahoma. The son of Kiowa Indians, Momaday won the Pulitzer Prize in 1969 for his book *House Made of Dawn*.

Bill Moyers (born 1934), a journalist from Hugo, Oklahoma, began his career as an assistant to President Lyndon B. Johnson. Moyers has worked for the PBS and CBS television networks and has won more than 30 Emmy Awards for his work.

Bill Moyers

Brad Pitt (born 1963) is a popular movie star who was born in Shawnee, Oklahoma. Known for his good looks, Pitt has starred in many movies, including *Twelve Monkeys*, *Fight Club*, and *Ocean's Eleven*.

Wiley Post (1899–1935) was the first pilot to fly around the world alone in an airplane. Post, born in Texas, grew up in Oklahoma. He and his friend Will Rogers were killed when Post's plane crashed in Alaska.

Wiley Post

Oral Roberts (born 1918), a preacher and missionary, was born near Ada, Oklahoma. Roberts preaches his religious beliefs in books, on the radio, on television, and at meetings all over the world. He founded Oral Roberts University in Tulsa.

Will Rogers

Will Rogers (1879–1935), born in Oologah, Oklahoma, wrote several books and a weekly newspaper column. He was also a world-famous actor, rope-trick artist, and comedian. Rogers, who was part Cherokee Indian, died in a plane crash in Alaska.

Dan Rowan (1922–1987), born in Beggs, Oklahoma, was a scriptwriter and television personality. Rowan is famous for his work on the television comedy show *Rowan & Martin's Laugh-In*, which aired on NBC from 1968 to 1973.

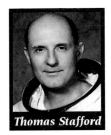

Thomas Stafford

Thomas Stafford (born 1930), an astronaut, has flown on four space missions, including one flight that orbited the moon. He is a member of the Astronaut Hall of Fame. Stafford was born in Weatherford, Oklahoma.

Willie Stargell (1940–2001) was a professional baseball player born in Earlsboro, Oklahoma. He played his entire career for the Pittsburgh Pirates (1962–1982), winning the World Series in 1971 and 1979. Stargell was elected to the National Baseball Hall of Fame in 1988.

Maria Tallchief

Maria Tallchief (born 1925) and **Marjorie Tallchief** (born 1927) were born in Fairfax, Oklahoma. Maria was the first lead ballerina of the New York City Ballet and founded the Chicago City Ballet in 1981. Marjorie was the solo ballerina for the Paris Opera Ballet Company for five years. The Tallchief sisters are part Osage.

Jim Thorpe

Jim Thorpe (1886–1953), a Sauk and Fox Indian born near Prague, Oklahoma, was sometimes called the best all-around athlete in the world. Thorpe won Olympic gold medals in track and field, was an outfielder for three baseball teams, and played professional football for 15 years.

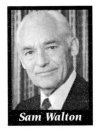

Sam Walton

Sam Walton (1918–1992) was the founder of Wal-Mart, a chain of stores known for their low prices. Born in Kingfisher, Oklahoma, Walton was one of the richest people in the United States.

FACTS-AT-A-GLANCE

Nickname: Sooner State

Song: "Oklahoma!"

Motto: *Labor Omnia Vincit*
(Labor Conquers All Things)

Flower: mistletoe

Tree: redbud

Bird: scissor-tailed flycatcher

Animal: buffalo

Reptile: collared lizard

Furbearer: raccoon

Musical instrument: fiddle

Date and ranking of statehood:
November 16, 1907, the 46th state

Capital: Oklahoma City

Area: 68,679 square miles

Rank in area, nationwide: 19

Average January temperature: 37° F

Average July temperature: 82° F

Oklahoma's flag shows seven eagle feathers and an Osage Indian shield. A peace pipe and an olive branch, two symbols of peace, cross in front of the shield.

POPULATION GROWTH

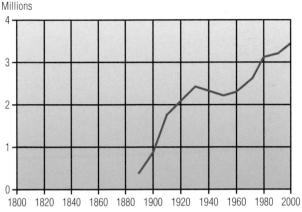

Millions

This chart shows how Oklahoma's population has changed from 1890 to 2000.

Oklahoma's state seal shows one large star surrounded by 45 smaller stars. The large star contains symbols of the five Indian groups that settled in Oklahoma in the 1830s. The smaller stars symbolize the states that made up the Union when Oklahoma became a state in 1907.

Population: 3,450,654 (2000 census)

Rank in population, nationwide: 27th

Major cities and populations: (2000 census) Oklahoma City (506,132), Tulsa (393,049), Norman (95,694), Lawton (92,757), Broken Arrow (74,859)

U.S. senators: 2

U.S. representatives: 5

Electoral votes: 7

Natural resources: coal, copper, fertile soil, granite, gypsum, natural gas, oil

Agricultural products: beef, chickens, corn, cotton, hay, hogs, peaches, peanuts, pecans, soybeans, watermelons, wheat

Manufactured goods: aircraft and aircraft parts, boilers, oil-field machinery, plastic products, pumps, refined oil, tires

WHERE OKLAHOMANS WORK

Services—60 percent (services includes jobs in trade; community, social, and personal services; finance, insurance, and real estate; transportation, communication, and utilities)

Government—16 percent

Manufacturing—10 percent

Agriculture—6 percent

Construction—5 percent

Mining—3 percent

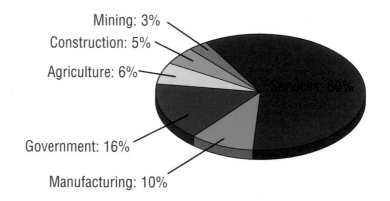

GROSS STATE PRODUCT

Services—56 percent

Manufacturing—17 percent

Government—16 percent

Mining—6 percent

Construction—3 percent

Agriculture—2 percent

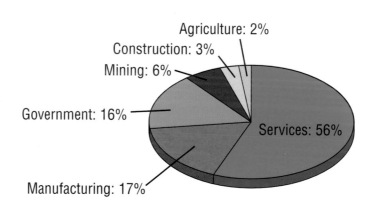

OKLAHOMA WILDLIFE

Mammals: antelope, armadillo, coyote, deer, fox, mink, opossum, prairie dog, rabbit, raccoon, squirrel

Birds: blue jay, cardinal, crow, dove, house sparrow, meadowlark, mockingbird, roadrunner, robin, scissor-tailed flycatcher

Reptiles and amphibians: copperhead snake, frogs, lizards, rattlesnake, salamanders, skink, toads, turtles

Fish: bass, buffalo fish, carp, catfish, crappie, drumfish, paddlefish, sunfish

Trees: ash, elm, hickory, oak, pecan, pine, redbud, sweet gum, walnut

Wild plants: anemone, black-eyed Susan, dogwood, goldenrod, mesquite, petunia, phlox, prairie grasses, primrose, sagebrush, spiderwort, sunflower, verbena, violet

Travelers in Oklahoma can spot road-runners along the state's roadsides.

PLACES TO VISIT

Cherokee Heritage Center, Tahlequah
The Trail of Tears ended in Tahlequah, and many Cherokee settled there. The Cherokee Heritage Center preserves their history. It includes Tsa-La-Gi Ancient Village, a re-creation of a Cherokee village of the 1500s, and Adams Corner Rural Village, a re-creation of a late 1800s Cherokee village.

Gilcrease Museum, Tulsa
This museum houses an impressive collection of western art. It features artwork by Frederic Remington, Charles M. Russell, and George Catlin. Other exhibits display North and South American archeological artifacts and Indian artifacts.

Grand Lake O' the Cherokees, northeastern Oklahoma
This lake is formed by the Pensacola Dam. Fishers, boaters, swimmers, and waterskiers flock to the third-largest lake in Oklahoma. State parks and resorts provide access to the lake.

Guthrie
Guthrie was the capital of Oklahoma until 1910, when many people left the town. Guthrie didn't change much after that— the town looks much as it did during the late 1800s and early 1900s. Visitors can explore its historic buildings and museums.

Little Sahara State Park, near Waynoka
This park is covered by about 1,500 acres of sand dunes. Some of the dunes are 75 feet high. Popular activities in the park include camping and riding off-road vehicles and dune buggies.

National Cowboy and Western Heritage Museum, Oklahoma City

Visitors get a feel for the history of the West through art and artifacts displayed at this museum. History and art exhibits honor Native Americans, cowboys, rodeo riders, and other important Western characters. The museum complex includes Prosperity Junction, an early 1900s western town.

Oklahoma City National Memorial

The victims of the 1995 Oklahoma City bombing are remembered here. The memorial is located on the site of the bombing. It includes a museum dedicated to the tragedy, classrooms for children, and an outdoor Symbolic Memorial.

Southern Plains Indian Museum, Anadarko

This museum displays historic Native American artifacts from Oklahoma, including clothing, weapons, and toys. Indian artists and craftspeople also show and sell their work.

Spiro Mounds Archaeological Park, near Spiro

Discovered by treasure hunters in the 1930s, this was a religious and trade center for Native Americans between 1100 and 1450. The twelve mounds on the site hold graves of religious leaders and other remains of the Spiro people. An interpretive center explains the importance of the site.

Will Rogers Memorial Museum, Claremore

A statue and a museum devoted to his life and times honor entertainer Will Rogers. Located in Rogers's hometown, the museum shows artwork, artifacts, and films related to Rogers.

ANNUAL EVENTS

International Finals Rodeo, Oklahoma City—*January*

World Championship Cow Chip Throwing Contest, Beaver—*April*

Pawnee Bill's Wild West Show, Pawnee—*June*

Red Earth Native American Cultural Festival, Oklahoma City—*June*

American Indian Exposition, Anadarko—*August*

Bullnanza, Oklahoma City—*August*

Jazz on Greenwood, Tulsa—*August*

Cherokee National Holiday, Tahlequah—*August–September*

Oklahoma State Fair, Oklahoma City—*September*

World Championship Quarter Horse Show, Oklahoma City—*November*

LEARN MORE ABOUT OKLAHOMA

BOOKS

General

Baldwin, Guy. *Oklahoma*. New York: Benchmark Books, 2001. For older readers.

Fradin, Dennis Brindell, and Judith Bloom Fradin. *Oklahoma*. Danbury, CT: Children's Press, 1995.

Special Interest

Coombs, Karen Mueller. *Children of the Dust Days*. Minneapolis, MN: Carolrhoda Books, Inc., 2000. The drought and dust storms of the 1930s hit Oklahoma hard. Through photos and text, this book examines the life of children in Oklahoma and other Great Plains states during these troubled times.

Kramer, Stephen. *Tornado*. Minneapolis, MN: Carolrhoda Books, Inc., 1992. Tornadoes strike Oklahoma often. Learn about kinds of tornadoes, how tornadoes form, where they happen, and how they are predicted.

Sherrow, Victoria. *The Oklahoma City Bombing: Terror in the Heartland*. Springfield, NJ: Enslow Publishers, Inc., 1998. Survivors of the Oklahoma City bombing describe the day of the tragedy. The book also discusses cleanup efforts, the search for the bombers, and the trials of Timothy McVeigh and Terry Nichols.

Stein, R. Conrad. *The Trail of Tears.* Chicago: Children's Press, 1993. Discusses the events leading up to the removal of the Cherokee and other Native American tribes from the eastern United States to what later became Oklahoma, as well as their difficult journey west.

Fiction

Antle, Nancy. *Beautiful Land: A Story of the Oklahoma Land Rush.* New York: Viking, 1996. Annie Mae's family has been waiting to claim land in the Oklahoma Territory. The family faces challenges during the Land Run of 1889 as they try to fulfill their dreams of owning farmland.

Porter, Tracy. *Treasures in the Dust.* New York: HarperCollins, 1997. Best friends Annie May and Violet live in Cimarron County, Oklahoma, during the Great Depression. The girls face the hardships of the Dust Bowl in different ways. For older readers.

Rawls, Wilson. *Where the Red Fern Grows.* New York: Delacorte Press, 1996. First published in 1961, this is the tale of a boy, Billy, growing up in the Ozark Mountains of Oklahoma. Billy works hard to buy a pair of hounds. Hunting raccoons with his beloved dogs, Old Dan and Little Ann, Billy has thrilling adventures. For older readers.

WEBSITES

Your Oklahoma
<http://www.state.ok.us/>
At the state's official website, viewers can find information about Oklahoma's government, businesses, history, and schools.

TravelOK
<http://travelok.com/>
Visit Oklahoma's official tourism website to plan an Oklahoma vacation. Learn about Oklahoma's cities, towns, festivals, parks, activities, and more.

NewsOK
<http://www.newsok.com/>
Keep up with Oklahoma events by reading an online version of the *Oklahoman*, an Oklahoma City daily newspaper.

PRONUNCIATION GUIDE

Cheyenne (shy-AN)

Chickasaw (CHIHK-uh-saw)

Choctaw (CHAHK-taw)

Comanche (kuh-MAN-chee)

Coronado, Francisco Vásquez de
  (kawr-uh-NAHD-oh, frahn-SIHS-koh
  BAHS-kayz day)

Kiowa (KY-uh-waw)

Osage (oh-SAYJ)

Ouachita (WAHSH-uh-taw)

Seminole (SEHM-uh-nohl)

Tahlequah (TAL-uh-kwaw)

Tsa-La-Gi (JAH-lah-gee)

Wichita (WHICH-uh-taw)

A stone marker indicates the spot where the boundaries of Oklahoma, Colorado, and New Mexico meet.

GLOSSARY

drought: a long period of extreme dryness due to lack of rain or snow

fossil fuel: a material such as coal or oil that is formed in the earth from the remains of ancient plants and animals. Fossil fuels are used to produce power.

geologist: a scientist who studies rocks to learn about the history of the earth

hydroelectric power: the electricity produced by using waterpower; also called hydropower

immigrant: a person who moves into a foreign country and settles there

mesa: an isolated hill with steep sides and a flat top

plantation: a large estate, usually in a warm climate, on which crops are grown by workers who live on the estate. In the past, plantation owners often used slave labor.

plateau: a large, relatively flat area that stands above the surrounding land

prairie: a large area of level or gently rolling grassy land with few trees

reservation: public land set aside by the government to be used by Native Americans

rural: having to do with the countryside or farming

urban: having to do with cities and large towns

INDEX

PHOTO ACKNOWLEDGMENTS

Cover photographs by © William A. Bake/CORBIS (left) and © Dave Bartruff/ CORBIS (right); PresentationMaps.com, pp. 1, 8, 9, 48; © Richard Hamilton Smith/CORBIS, pp. 2–3; © Steve Vidler/SuperStock, p. 3; © Wolfgang Kaehler/CORBIS, pp. 4 (detail), 7 (detail), 17 (detail), 39 (detail), 51 (detail); © David Vinyard/Photo Network, p. 6; Al Myatt, Area Forester, Oklahoma Department of Agriculture/Forestry Services, pp. 7, 50; Oklahoma Tourism/Fred W. Marvel, pp. 10, 13, 15, 18, 40, 42, 44 (both), 45 (both), 46, 47, 80; Harvey Payne, pp. 11 (both), 12, 54; © 1992 NOAA/Weatherstock, p. 14; Outdoor Oklahoma, the official publication of the Oklahoma Department of Wildlife Conservation, p. 16 (both); Independent Picture Service, pp. 17, 66 (bottom), 67 (second from top); Annette Hume, Oklahoma Historical Society, p. 19 (#14998); Library of Congress, pp. 20, 26, 34; The Philbrook Museum of Art, Tulsa, Oklahoma, p. 22; Western History Collections, University of Oklahoma Library, pp. 23, 27, 28, 37; Jos. Hitchens, Oklahoma Historical Society, p. 24 (#16575); Oklahoma Historical Society, pp. 25 (#8687), 31 (#19389), 33 (#15583.B); Oklahoma Territorial Museum, Oklahoma Historical Society, p. 29 (both); George W. Parsons, Mitscher Collection, Oklahoma Historical Society, p. 32 (#3191.5); G. L. R., Oklahoma Historical Society, p. 35 (#16575); © AFP/CORBIS, p. 38; Mike King, p. 39; © Richard Jacobs/Root Resources, p. 41; © Scott Berner/Visuals Unlimited, p. 43; McDonnell Douglas, p. 49; © William J. Weber/Visuals Unlimited, p. 52; Apache Corp., American Petroleum Institute, p. 53; © George D. Lepp/CORBIS, p. 55; Oklahoma State Department of Health, p. 56; Everett Krute, Sand Springs, OK, p. 57; © Tom Bean/CORBIS, p. 58; Jack Lindstrom, p. 60; Shauna Plyler/Durant Chamber of Commerce, p. 61; Tim Seeley, pp. 63, 71 (top), 72; Division of Manuscripts, University of Oklahoma Library, p. 66 (top); Bern Schwartz, p. 66 (middle); © Mitchell Gerber/CORBIS, p. 67 (top); Cherokee Nation of Oklahoma, p. 67 (second from bottom); Stew Thornley, p. 67 (bottom); Linda Fry Poverman, p. 68 (top); © Chase Roe/Retna Ltd., p. 68 (second from top); Lockheed, p. 68 (second from bottom); Station KSTP, Minneapolis, p. 68 (bottom); NASA, p. 69 (top); Chicago City Ballet, p. 69 (second from top); Pro Football Hall of Fame, p. 69 (second from bottom); Wal-Mart Stores, Inc., p. 69 (bottom); Jean Matheny, p. 70 (top); © Joe McDonald/CORBIS, p. 73.